Practicing for *Success*

STAAR
Writing

Grade 4

Publishing Credits

Rachelle Cracchiolo, M.S.Ed., *Publisher;* Conni Medina, M.A.Ed., *Managing Editor;* Aubrie Nielsen, M.S.Ed., *Series Developer;* Véronique Bos, *Creative Director;* Robin Erickson, *Art Director;* Lee Aucoin, *Senior Graphic Designer;* Don Tran, *Graphic Designer;* Tara Hurley, *Assistant Editor*

Contributing Author

Jordana Benone, M.A.Ed.

Consultant

Kim Carlton, M.Ed.
Academic Officer, Texas

Image Credits

Noted graphics and visuals provided by *TIME For Kids. TIME For Kids* and the *TIME For Kids* logo are registered trademarks of TIME Inc.

All other images are from Shutterstock.com or iStock.com, unless otherwise noted.

Standards

© Copyright 2007–2017 Texas Education Agency (TEA). All Rights Reserved.

The TIME For Kids logo is a registered trademark of TIME For Kids Inc. Used under license.
To order TIME For Kids magazine, contact:
TIME For Kids
1-800-777-8600
www.timeforkids.com/subscribe

Teacher Created Materials

5301 Oceanus Drive
Huntington Beach, CA 92649-1030
www.tcmpub.com

ISBN 978-1-4938-8577-0

© 2018 Teacher Created Materials, Inc.

Table of Contents

Student Welcome

Dear Student,

Welcome to *Practicing for Success!* This book will prepare you for the State of Texas Assessments of Academic Readiness (STAAR). When you have completed this book, you will be more prepared for the STAAR exam!

The exercises in this book will help you practice your test-taking skills. The exercises look similar to the questions on the STAAR test, so you will know what to expect when you take this annual assessment in the spring. The exercises will test you on what you have been learning in school. If you begin these practice exercises early in the school year, they may seem difficult or there may be things you do not know well. But later in the year, after you have learned more in your class and you have had more practice taking tests, you should find that the practice exercises are more familiar and that you feel more confident in your answers.

These practice exercises will give you a good idea of what to expect on the STAAR. The exercises will show you how much you already know, and they will show you what you need to work on in order to succeed. If you pay attention to the questions you answer incorrectly on the practice exercises, you can see what kinds of questions you need to practice more. Then, you can improve your skills to help you succeed on the STAAR exam.

The following tips will help you as you complete the practice exercises:

- Listen to your teacher's instructions. They will provide important information and helpful tips.
- Read all directions closely. Underline or circle details in the questions to help you focus on what is being asked.
- When answering multiple-choice questions, read every answer carefully. Cross out answers you know are incorrect to help you find the correct answer.
- After you complete the practice questions, go back and check your answers.

We hope that this book will help you feel ready to take the STAAR test. With practice and hard work, you will be ready to succeed on test day!

Name: _____ Date: _____

Practice Composition: Being Different

READ the information in the box below.

> "Embrace your uniqueness. Time is much too short to be living someone else's life."
>
> — Kobi Yamada, author

THINK about the things that make you unique and different from everyone else.

WRITE about one thing that makes you different from everyone else. Describe it in detail, and explain why it makes you unique.

Make sure that you —

- state your central idea
- keep your writing organized
- use details to support your writing
- carefully consider your word choice
- write with accurate spelling, correct grammar, and appropriate capitalization and punctuation

Name: _____ Date: _____

```
┌─────────────────────────────────────────────────────┐
│     USE THIS PAGE TO PLAN YOUR COMPOSITION.           │
│     WRITE YOUR COMPOSITION ON A LINED PAGE.           │
└─────────────────────────────────────────────────────┘
```

USE THIS PAGE TO PLAN YOUR COMPOSITION.
WRITE YOUR COMPOSITION ON A LINED PAGE.

Name: _____ Date: _____

_____
_____
_____
_____
_____
_____
_____
_____
_____
_____
_____
_____
_____
_____
_____
_____
_____
_____
_____
_____
_____
_____
_____
_____
_____
_____
_____

STUDENTS MAY NOT WRITE OUTSIDE THE BOX

STOP

© *Teacher Created Materials*

Name: _____ Date: _____

Practice Composition: Food

READ the information in the box below.

> You are what you eat.

THINK about the things you like to eat and things you don't care to eat.

WRITE about one thing you like to eat and one thing you don't like to eat. Explain why you like and dislike them.

Make sure that you —

- state your central idea
- keep your writing organized
- use details to support your writing
- carefully consider your word choice
- write with accurate spelling, correct grammar, and appropriate capitalization and punctuation

Name: _____ Date: _____

USE THIS PAGE TO PLAN YOUR COMPOSITION.
WRITE YOUR COMPOSITION ON A LINED PAGE.

© *Teacher Created Materials*

Name: _____ Date: _____

```
┌──────────────────────────────────────────────┐
│   USE THIS PAGE TO PLAN YOUR COMPOSITION.      │
│   WRITE YOUR COMPOSITION ON A LINED PAGE.      │
└──────────────────────────────────────────────┘
```

Name: _____ Date: _____

STOP

100506—TIME For Kids Practicing for Success: STAAR

© *Teacher Created Materials*

Practice Composition: Keeping the Planet Clean

READ the information in the box below.

> Everyone needs to lend a hand in making the planet pollution free.

THINK about what kids can do to take care of the planet to keep it pollution free.

WRITE about one thing kids can do to keep the planet pollution free. Explain why it is important.

Make sure that you —

- state your central idea
- keep your writing organized
- use details to support your writing
- carefully consider your word choice
- write with accurate spelling, correct grammar, and appropriate capitalization and punctuation

GO ON

Name: _____ Date: _____

```
┌──────────────────────────────────────────────────┐
│  USE THIS PAGE TO PLAN YOUR COMPOSITION.           │
│  WRITE YOUR COMPOSITION ON A LINED PAGE.           │
└──────────────────────────────────────────────────┘
```

Name: _____ Date: _____

```
┌─────────────────────────────────────────┐
│  USE THIS PAGE TO PLAN YOUR COMPOSITION.  │
│  WRITE YOUR COMPOSITION ON A LINED PAGE.  │
└─────────────────────────────────────────┘
```

Name: _____ Date: _____

Name: _____   Date: _____

Practice Composition: Outdoor Fun

READ the information in the box below.

> Outdoor activities are a great way to have a good time with your friends or your family.

THINK about activities you like to do outdoors.

WRITE about one activity you like to do outside, and explain why you like it.

Make sure that you —

- state your central idea
- keep your writing organized
- use details to support your writing
- carefully consider your word choice
- write with accurate spelling, correct grammar, and appropriate capitalization and punctuation

GO ON

Name: _____ Date: _____

```
┌─────────────────────────────────────────────────┐
│  USE THIS PAGE TO PLAN YOUR COMPOSITION.          │
│  WRITE YOUR COMPOSITION ON A LINED PAGE.          │
└─────────────────────────────────────────────────┘
```

Name: _____ Date: _____

USE THIS PAGE TO PLAN YOUR COMPOSITION.
WRITE YOUR COMPOSITION ON A LINED PAGE.

Name: _____ Date: _____

STUDENTS MAY NOT WRITE OUTSIDE THE BOX

STOP

Practice Composition: Nighttime Routine

READ the information in the box below.

> "Though sleep is called our best friend, it is a friend who often keeps us waiting!"
>
> — Jules Verne, author

THINK about your nighttime routine and the kinds of things you like to do to fall asleep.

WRITE a description of one thing that you like to do before going to bed. Explain why you like this nighttime routine.

Make sure that you —

- state your central idea
- keep your writing organized
- use details to support your writing
- carefully consider your word choice
- write with accurate spelling, correct grammar, and appropriate capitalization and punctuation

Name: _____ Date: _____

```
┌─────────────────────────────────────────────────────┐
│        USE THIS PAGE TO PLAN YOUR COMPOSITION.        │
│        WRITE YOUR COMPOSITION ON A LINED PAGE.        │
└─────────────────────────────────────────────────────┘
```

Name: _____ Date: _____

> USE THIS PAGE TO PLAN YOUR COMPOSITION.
> WRITE YOUR COMPOSITION ON A LINED PAGE.

Name: _____ Date: _____

Name: _____ Date: _____

Practice Composition: Free Time

READ the information in the box below.

> "All we have to decide is what to do with the time that is given to us."
>
> — Gandalf
> *The Fellowship of the Ring* by J.R.R. Tolkien

THINK about the activities you like to do in your free time.

WRITE about one activity you like to do in your free time. Explain why you like this activity.

Make sure that you —

- state your central idea
- keep your writing organized
- use details to support your writing
- carefully consider your word choice
- write with accurate spelling, correct grammar, and appropriate capitalization and punctuation

Name: _____ Date: _____

```
┌─────────────────────────────────────────────────┐
│   USE THIS PAGE TO PLAN YOUR COMPOSITION.         │
│   WRITE YOUR COMPOSITION ON A LINED PAGE.         │
└─────────────────────────────────────────────────┘
```

Name: _____ Date: _____

USE THIS PAGE TO PLAN YOUR COMPOSITION.
WRITE YOUR COMPOSITION ON A LINED PAGE.

Name: _____ Date: _____

Name: _____ Date: _____

Practice Composition: Saving Money

READ the information in the box below.

> A penny saved is a penny earned.

THINK about reasons why it is a good idea to save money and not spend it all. Imagine something for which you would like to save money.

WRITE about something you would like to save money for. Explain what it is and why you want to save for it.

Make sure that you —

- state your central idea
- keep your writing organized
- use details to support your writing
- carefully consider your word choice
- write with accurate spelling, correct grammar, and appropriate capitalization and punctuation

Name: _____ Date: _____

USE THIS PAGE TO PLAN YOUR COMPOSITION.
WRITE YOUR COMPOSITION ON A LINED PAGE.

Name: _____ Date: _____

USE THIS PAGE TO PLAN YOUR COMPOSITION.
WRITE YOUR COMPOSITION ON A LINED PAGE.

Name: _____ Date: _____

Name: _____ Date: _____

Practice Composition: Home

READ the information in the box below.

> As Dorothy says in the movie *The Wizard of Oz*, "There's no place like home."

THINK about your community, your town, or your city.

WRITE about what you like best about your neighborhood or your community. Explain why it is your favorite thing.

Make sure that you —

- state your central idea
- keep your writing organized
- use details to support your writing
- carefully consider your word choice
- write with accurate spelling, correct grammar, and appropriate capitalization and punctuation

Name: _____ Date: _____

> USE THIS PAGE TO PLAN YOUR COMPOSITION.
> WRITE YOUR COMPOSITION ON A LINED PAGE.

Name: _____ Date: _____

> USE THIS PAGE TO PLAN YOUR COMPOSITION.
> WRITE YOUR COMPOSITION ON A LINED PAGE.

Name: _____ Date: _____

Name: _____   Date: _____

Practice Composition: Chores

READ the information in the box below.

> Families need to work together to create a happy home.

THINK about the ways you help around your home.

WRITE about one way you help around your home. Describe what you do and why it's helpful.

Make sure that you —

- state your central idea
- keep your writing organized
- use details to support your writing
- carefully consider your word choice
- write with accurate spelling, correct grammar, and appropriate capitalization and punctuation

Name: _____ Date: _____

```
┌─────────────────────────────────────────────────┐
│    USE THIS PAGE TO PLAN YOUR COMPOSITION.        │
│    WRITE YOUR COMPOSITION ON A LINED PAGE.        │
└─────────────────────────────────────────────────┘
```

Name: _____ Date: _____

> USE THIS PAGE TO PLAN YOUR COMPOSITION.
> WRITE YOUR COMPOSITION ON A LINED PAGE.

Name: _____ Date: _____

Name: _____ Date: _____

Practice Composition: Water

READ the information in the box below.

> Water is a precious resource in our world.

THINK about why water is so important in your life. Consider the ways you try to be responsible with water in your everyday life.

WRITE about one way you try to be responsible with water usage. Explain why this is important.

Make sure that you —

- state your central idea
- keep your writing organized
- use details to support your writing
- carefully consider your word choice
- write with accurate spelling, correct grammar, and appropriate capitalization and punctuation

Name: _____ Date: _____

> USE THIS PAGE TO PLAN YOUR COMPOSITION.
> WRITE YOUR COMPOSITION ON A LINED PAGE.

Name: _____ Date: _____

```
┌─────────────────────────────────────────────────┐
│   USE THIS PAGE TO PLAN YOUR COMPOSITION.         │
│   WRITE YOUR COMPOSITION ON A LINED PAGE.         │
└─────────────────────────────────────────────────┘
```

Name: _____ Date: _____

Name: _____   Date: _____

The Supersize U.S.?

Directions: Read the selection and respond to the questions on pages 47–48.

Jose wrote this essay to explain what he learned about problems with obesity in the United States. Jose would like you to read his essay and find any corrections that need to be made. When you finish reading, answer the questions that follow.

(1) The United States has a supersize problem. (2) Many Americans weigh too much! (3) More than half of all grown-ups weigh more than they should. (4) Not only that, the problem seems to be getting worse.

(5) The Centers for Disease Control and Prevention (CDC) estimates that about 64% of adults are overweight or obese. (6) Today, there are twice as many overweight adults as there were 20 years ago. (7) There are about 9 million children who are dangerously overweight.

(8) Doctors are worried about this growing problems. (9) Being very overweight is serious. (10) It can cause heart disease, diabetes, and other health problems. (11) Type 2 diabetes, once considered an adult disease, has increased in young people.

(12) Clearly this is a dangerous trend. (13) How did so many people get out of shape? (14) The U.S. Department of Health and Human Services says that nearly half of all children do not get enough physical activity. (15) At the same time, health experts say, children are eating more and more junk food.

The Supersize U.S.? *(cont.)*

(16) Nancy Krebs is a doctor who works with kids. (17) She says kids spend too much time watching TV. (18) They don't spend enough time being active and playing sports. (19) On top of that, Americans are eating out more than ever. (20) Fast food and pizza are very fattening. (21) Plus, the meal sizes are often too big.

(22) Some fast-food companies are now offering meals that are lower in fat. (23) Public schools are trying to serve meals that are more healthful. (24) In 2003, the government bought more than 973 million pounds of fruits and vegetables for schools!

(25) Parents and kids are also making changes. (26) Danielle Bailey, age 7, took part in the KidShape program in California. (27) "It taught me to eat more carrots, strawberries, and grapes," she says. (28) I also learned to go for more walks in the park."

(29) Can anything stop the supersizing of America? (30) It's a big problem, but as Danielle learned, if we eat the right way and play the right way, we will way right.

GO ON

The Supersize U.S.? *(cont.)*

1   The central idea of Jose's paper is weak. Which of the following would be the **BEST** sentence to add just before sentence 3 to provide a better central idea for this essay?

   A   Research has shown that kids who are more physically fit do better in school.

   B   Another problem is that overweight kids can often be targets of bullying or name calling.

   C   Doctors and scientists are worried about kids becoming overweight because it may lead to health issues such as heart disease, diabetes, asthma, sleep problems, and bullying.

   D   Studies have shown that overweight kids are likely to become overweight grown-ups.

---

2   What change should be made in sentence 8?

   F   Change *are* to **is**

   G   Change *this* to **that**

   H   Change *Doctors* to **Doctor**

   J   Change *problems* to **problem**

---

3   Jose needs more supporting details that show how serious the problem is. Which of these sentences **BEST** follows sentence 11?

   A   Another problem is that overweight kids can often be targets of bullying or name calling.

   B   Research has shown that kids who are more physically fit do better in school.

   C   There are many steps kids can take to become more physically fit.

   D   Even though there is a lot of research, figuring out what is a healthy weight for kids can be challenging.

The Supersize U.S.? *(cont.)*

4 What change, if any, should be made in sentence 28?

    F Insert quotation marks at the beginning of the sentence

    G Insert a comma after *learned*

    H Remove the quotation marks at the end of the sentence

    J Make no change

---

5 How should sentence 30 be changed?

    A Change *It's* to **Its**

    B Change the first *right* to **write**

    C Change the third *way* to **weigh**

    D Sentence 30 should not be changed.

---

6 What change, if any, should be made in sentence 30 to better describe the kind of problem this is?

    F Change *problem* to **situation**

    G Change *learned* to **knew**

    H Change *big* to **crazy**

    J Make no change

Name: _____ Date: _____

Hooked on Oil

Directions: Read the selection and respond to the questions on pages 51–52.

Emily's teacher had the class write essays on problems with the environment. Emily did research and wrote this essay on oil. She would like you to read the essay and help her identify any mistakes. After you are finished reading, answer the questions that follow.

(1) Deep beneath Earth's surface, oil lies in shiny, sticky pools. (2) Oil powers cars, factories, trains, planes, and electrical plants.

(3) Some nashuns have vast underground lakes of oil. (4) Other places, such as Japan and most European nations, have little oil of their own. (5) The nations that need oil must buy it from oil-rich nations. (6) Four countries—Saudi arabia, Iraq, Iran, and Russia—control almost 70% of the world's oil.

(7) The U.S. uses more oil than any other nation. (8) Most of it is pumped into 200 million cars and trucks as gasoline. (9) On average, each American uses 25 barrels of oil a year. (10) Compare this with 15 barrels for someone in Japan or 12 for someone in France.

Hooked on Oil (cont.)

(11) The U.S. may use a lot of it, but oil is one messy fuel. (12) When fosil fuels burn, they send off carbon dioxide and other polluting gases into the air. (13) These gases can harm our health and our planet. (14) They can trap heat near Earth's surface. (15) This can lead to rising temperatures, a process called "global warming." (16) Plus, some ships carrying oil have spilled millions of gallons of oil into the water. (17) These spills pollute our oceans and kill sea life.

(18) In the 1970s, oil prices rose. In response, new rules forced auto manufacturers to build cars that used less gas. (19) In 1975, the average car went 12 miles on a gallon of gas. (20) By 1990, some got 30 miles per gallon. (21) But in recent years, as oil prices went down, Americans went back to buying gas-guzzlers. (22) About one of every four cars now sold is a sport utility vehicle (SUV). (23) These cars get as little as 10 or 11 miles per gallon.

(24) What is the solution to our oil habit? (25) Smaller cars? (26) Better gas mileage? (27) Drilling for oil in wilderness areas? (28) New sources of energy such as wind and sunlight? (29) Its a problem, and stickier it gets as time goes by. (30) Let's hope we have the energy to solve it.

Hooked on Oil *(cont.)*

1   How does sentence 3 need to be changed?

   A   Change *underground* to **undergrounds**

   B   Change *nashuns* to **nations**

   C   Change *lakes* to **lakies**

   D   No change is needed.

---

2   How does sentence 6 need to be changed?

   F   Change *countries* to **Countries**

   G   Change *Iraq* to **iraq**

   H   Change *Saudi arabia* to **Saudi Arabia**

   J   Change *world's* to **World's**

---

3   What change should be made in sentence 12?

   A   Change *polluting* to **poluting**

   B   Change *fuels* to **fools**

   C   Change *fosil* to **fossil**

   D   Change *gases* to **gasses**

Hooked on Oil *(cont.)*

4 Emily needs to use an appropriate transition at the beginning of sentence 24. Which of the following transitions should be added before sentence 24?

    F For example,

    G So,

    H Furthermore,

    J Also,

---

5 What is the correct way to write sentence 29?

    A It's a problem that gets stickier as time goes by.

    B It's a problem, and it gets stickier when time goes by.

    C As time goes by it's a problem, it get stickier.

    D Make no change

---

6 Emily would like to add a sentence to the last paragraph (sentences 24–30) to support the fact that there are ideas people are working on to improve the oil situation. Which of the following would be the **BEST** sentence to add just before sentence 29?

    F These are some ideas that scientists and inventors are exploring to solve the problem.

    G Maybe there are some more ideas that can help besides just these.

    H What kinds of things can you do at home to help?

    J Many cities have solar powered buildings.

Name: _____   Date: _____

A Frozen Vacation with Bragging Rights

Directions: Read the selection and respond to the questions on pages 55–56.

Jacob's teacher asked the class to research and write about an interesting place to vacation. Jacob needs you to read his essay about vacationing in the North Pole to see if he made any mistakes. When you are finished reading, answer the questions that follow.

(1) How would you like to go on vacation to a place that's cold and bleak? (2) A place where you have to keep an eye out for polar bears. (3) Does that sound like fun? (4) Then a vacation at the North Pole is for you!

(5) Yes, more and more people are picking the North Pole as their vacation spot. (6) Getting there is hard and expensive. (7) And their is not much to do when you arrive. (8) But that just seems to give visitors more to brag about when they return home.

(9) About 200 tourists go to the North Pole each year. (10) Just about anyone can do it, as long as you're ready to pay the fare. (11) A vacation there costs between $12,000 and $15,000. (12) Most people travel by helicopter to Camp Barneo. (13) The camp is a collection of heated red and yellow tents about 60 miles from the Pole. (14) Since there's no land at the North Pole, on a floating ice pack is where Camp Barneo is. (15) The tourist season is in early spring. (16) In spring, the sun never sets north of the Arctic Circle. (17) That means it's always daylight at the camp.

A Frozen Vacation with Bragging Rights *(cont.)*

(18) There's a mess hall, where the cooking equipment consists of microwave ovens and a coffee machine. (19) Conditions are still much better than those faced by early explorers, many of whom died trying to get to the Pole on foot. (20) Today, only a few adventurers still arrive at Camp Barneo on skis.

(21) However, many do try to ski the last 60 miles to the Pole. (22) Those who don't feel like skiing can take another helicopter ride to the Pole. (23) One group of Rushan skydivers parachuted there.

(24) It's hard to tell exactly where the Pole is, since the ice keeps moving and compasses are useless that far north. (25) The only way to be sure you're at the Pole is to use a satellite signal. (26) Some tourists is disappointed to find there's nothing at the Pole but ice and more ice. (27) But at least visitors come home with a photo. (28) Then they can tell their friends, "See, I was at the North Pole!"

GO ON

A Frozen Vacation with Bragging Rights *(cont.)*

1 What change, if any, needs to be made in sentence 7?

   A Change *do* to **due**

   B Change *not* to **knot**

   C Change *their* to **there**

   D Make no change

---

2 Jacob forgot to include the following sentence in the third paragraph (sentences 9–17).

> *The strong winds make the ice pack drift, so Camp Barneo has to be rebuilt from scratch every year.*

Reread the paragraph carefully. Where is the **BEST** place to insert this sentence?

   F After sentence 14

   G After sentence 17

   H After sentence 9

   J After sentence 12

---

3 The meaning of sentence 14 is unclear. Which of the following would be the **BEST** way for Jacob to rewrite sentence 14?

   A Since there's no land at the North Pole, Camp Barneo sits on a floating ice pack.

   B On a floating ice pack is where Camp Barneo sits since there's no land at the North Pole.

   C Since there's no land at the North Pole, in a floating ice pack is where Camp Barneo is.

   D At the North Pole there's no land, so on a floating ice pack is where Camp Barneo is.

A Frozen Vacation with Bragging Rights *(cont.)*

4 What adjective needs to be added to sentence 20 to better describe the adventurers?

    F nice

    G rugged

    H easy

    J difficult

---

5 What change needs to be made in sentence 23?

    A Change *parachuted* to **parashuted**

    B Change *parachuted* to **parassiuted**

    C Change *Rushan* to **Rucian**

    D Change *Rushan* to **Russian**

---

6 What change, if any, needs to be made in sentence 26?

    F Change *is* to **are**

    G Change *there's* to **there are**

    H Change *tourists* to **tourist**

    J Make no change

Name: _____ Date: _____

Four Hurricanes in a Row

Directions: Read the selection and respond to the questions on pages 59–60.

Mia's class just finished learning about hurricanes. Mia wrote this essay after doing research on some of the worst hurricanes in U.S. history. Mia would like you to read the essay and look for any errors. After you are done reading, answer the questions that follow.

(1) Like four runaway trains, four hurricanes hit Florida one after the other in 2004. (2) First came Charley, which arrived August 13. (3) Charley rolled across the state from the Gulf of Mexico. (4) Then on September 5, Hurricane Frances hit the Atlantic coast heading west. (5) Frances had a mind of its own. (6) After it left Florida, it came back again. (7) Just 11 days later, Hurricane Ivan landed on the Florida panhandle with winds of more than 100 miles an hour. (8) Then, Hurricane Jeanne pounded Florida near the end of September. (9) It hit the coast near where Frances struck.

(10) It's hard to imagine the force of these storms. (11) Charley, for example, was packing winds as strong as 145 mile per hour. (12) Frances was strong enough to rip off roofs, smash boats, and tear trees out, roots and all. (13) Highways were washed away, homes and stores flooded.

Four Hurricanes in a Row *(cont.)*

(14) These rain-soaked steamrollers left an unbelievable amount of damage in their path. (15) At least 70 people were killed and billions of dollars worth of property was destroyed. (16) The damage was especially terrible in mobile home parks, where hundreds of thousands of Florida residents, many of them retirees, live.

(17) Late summer and fall have always been hurricane season. (18) Still, only once before has one state been hit by four hurricanes in the same year. (19) The residents of Florida were weary. (20) It was like being hit over and over by a string of boxers.

(21) Why so many big storms? Scientists think higher ocean temperatures had something to do with it. (22) In the mid-1990s, surface temperatures in the Atlantic increased 1°F to 1.5°F. (23) This rise in water temperature is a result of shifting ocean currents. (24) The last time the Atlantic warmed, between 1926 and 1970, a slew of dangerous storms hit the coast.

(25) Of course, knowing the cause of the storms was not much comfort to the shell-shocked people of Florida. (26) All they could do was try to pick up the pieces and hope that the last of the whirlwinds had come and gone.

Four Hurricanes in a Row *(cont.)*

1 Mia forgot to include an important detail in the first paragraph (sentences 1–9).

> *Even though more storms hit Florida than any other U.S. state, 2004 was an exceptionally bad year.*

Reread the paragraph carefully. Where is the **BEST** place to insert this sentence?

A Before sentence 6

B Before sentence 9

C After sentence 1

D After sentence 9

---

2 What change needs to be made in sentence 7?

F Change *panhandle* to **Panhandle**

G Change *Hurricane* to **hurricane**

H Change *Ivan* to **ivan**

J Change *miles an hour* to **Miles an Hour**

---

3 What word can be used instead of *Then* in sentence 8 to **BEST** show that Hurricane Jeanne was the last of the four hurricanes to hit?

A Next

B Finally

C Afterward

D No change is needed in sentence 8.

GO ON

Four Hurricanes in a Row *(cont.)*

4   What change, if any, needs to be made in sentence 11?

    F   Change *was* to **were**

    G   Change *hour* to **hours**

    H   Change *mile* to **miles**

    J   No change needs to be made.

---

5   What change can Mia make to sentence 20 to better describe the effect of the hurricanes?

    A   Change *string* to **group**

    B   Change *boxers* to **people**

    C   Change *by* to **with**

    D   Change *hit* to **punched**

---

6   What change, if any, should be made in sentence 23?

    F   Change *temperature* to **temperachure**

    G   Change *ocean* to **lake**

    H   Change *rise* to **fall**

    J   No change needs to be made in this sentence.

Name: _____ Date: _____

Coyote and Blue Fox

A Tale of the Pueblo People of the Southwest

Directions: Read the selection and respond to the questions on pages 63–64.

Joshua wrote a retelling of this folktale for a storytelling contest. Before he shows his teacher, he needs you to read it to see if you can help him find any mistakes. When you are done reading, answer the questions that follow.

(1) Once upon a time, Little Blue Fox was walking by the pueblo when he saw Coyote coming.

(2) "Little Blue Fox," Coyote cried, "you are always getting me in trouble. (3) You get the dogs to chase me. (4) You show the people where to hunt me. (5) I am sick of it."

(6) Little Blue Fox was not as big or as fast as Coyote. (7) He had to think fast. (8) "Okay, Coyote," he said. (9) "But than I won't be able to take you to the dance in the pueblo."

(10) "What dance?" Coyote asked, stopping in his tracks.

GO ON

Coyote and Blue Fox *(cont.)*

(11) "The drum will be beating soon," Little Blue Fox said. (12) "I have been asked to dance, and I was going to take you with me."

(13) "Great," Coyote said. (14) "Let's go!"

(15) "I'd better go first," Little Blue Fox said, "to make sure the people don't chase you." (16) Little Blue Fox disappeared into the pueblo. (17) Meanwhile, Coyote got ready for the dance. (18) He brushed his teeth, combed his hair, and put on face paint. (19) Soon, the people came out of the pueblo.

(20) "Oh, they're coming to take me to the dance!" Coyote thought. (21) But of course, they weren't. (22) The people all began to chase Coyote. (23) He ran for his life. (24) A little while later, Little Blue Fox apeared to Coyote again. (25) He was standing by a cliff in the desert. (26) Again, Little Blue Fox had to think fast. (27) Before Coyote got to him, he stood up and put his paws on the cliff.

(28) Coyote ran up. (29) "I've got you this time!" he cried.

(30) "Oh, Coyote!" Little Blue Fox said. (31) "This cliff are about to fall over. (32) It will crush us both if we don't hold it up." (33) Quickly, Coyote stood up with his paws against the cliff.

(34) "Oh, thank you," Little Blue Fox said. (35) Then Little Blue Fox said, "Coyote, we need a big stick to hold up this cliff. (36) I will go and look for one."

(37) "Okay," Coyote said. (38) "But hurry up."

(39) Of course, Little Blue Fox did hurry. (40) He hurried away as fast as he could. (41) As for Coyote, he's still standing there, holding up that cliff!

(42) Moral: Fool me once, shame on you. (43) Fool me twice, shame on me.

Name: _____ Date: _____

Coyote and Blue Fox (cont.)

1 Joshua needs to use a word other than ***walking*** in sentence 1 of his story because it is not very descriptive. Which of the following is the **BEST** replacement for the word *walking* in sentence 1?

  A jogging

  B moving

  C strolling

  D skipping

---

2 The story's central idea is that Little Blue Fox tricks the big, strong coyote because Coyote is dangerous. Which of the following could be added after sentence 5 to make the central idea stronger?

  F I am going to eat you!

  G You make me mad!

  H Why do you always trick me?

  J It's not nice to play tricks!

---

3 What change, if any, is needed in sentence 9?

  A Change ***take*** to **follow**

  B Change ***But*** to **And**

  C Change ***than*** to **then**

  D No change should be made.

Name: _____ Date: _____

Coyote and Blue Fox *(cont.)*

4   What change, if any, needs to be made in sentence 18?

    F   Change *teeth* to **tooths**

    G   Change *hair* to **hairs**

    H   Change *paint* to **paints**

    J   No change needs to be made.

---

5   What change should be made in sentence 24?

    A   Change *later* to **latter**

    B   Change *apeared* to **appeared**

    C   Change *little* to **litle**

    D   No change should be made.

---

6   What change needs to be made to sentence 31?

    F   Change *are* to **is**

    G   Change *This* to **These**

    H   Change *fall* to **falls**

    J   Make no change

Name: _____ Date: _____

Two Bike Mechanics

Directions: Read the selection and respond to the questions on pages 67–68.

Madison wrote this story after learning about the Wright brothers in school. She would like you to read it and find any mistakes. After you are done, answer the questions that follow.

(1) Lester hurried down Third Street. (2) He could hardly keep himself from running. (3) Today was the day!

(4) The 12-year-old grabbed his cap and looked up and down the busy street. (5) As soon as the trolley passed, he rushed across. (6) There it was, the Wright Brothers' Bicycle Shop. (7) The Wright brothers built the best bicycles in Dayton, Ohio. (8) Now Lester was going to own one, a red Fleetwing! (9) He'd been paying four dollars a week for the past nine weeks. (10) He pushed open the big double doors to the shop and enter.

(11) "Lester! I was just wondering when you'd show up," said a man behind the counter. (12) He was skinny and stood about five feet seven inches tall. (13) He had a thick mustache, and his head was covered with curly brown hair. (14) The man's gray-blue eyes twinkled as he looked at the boy.

(15) "Here it is, Mr. Wright," Lester said. (16) He placed his money on the counter. (17) "The last payment."

Name: _____   Date: _____

(18) Orville Wright wiped his hands on his blue-and-white-striped apron. (19) He took the bills and counted them out slowly.

(20) "Two, three, four. (21) That makes 40 dollars, exactly," he said. (22) "Wilbur!" he called. (23) "We've just sold another bicycle."

(24) Orville's older brother came in from the workroom. (25) Wilbur Wright was slightly taller, and he was almost totaly bald. (26) He carried something that looked like a large kite.

(27) "Oh, is that the glider you're working on?" Lester asked.

(28) "A model of it," Wilbur answered.

(29) "We've got the real thing in the back," Orville said. (30) "Want to see it?"

(31) "Sure," Lester answered. (32) Then he remembered the Fleetwing. (33) "Uh, but what about my bike?"

(34) Orville laughed. (35) "Of course, first things first!"

(36) Wilbur rolled the gleaming red bike into the showroom. (37) Lester grabbed it. (38) He could hardly wait to ride it. (39) Orville held the front door open as the boy wheeled the bike out onto the sidewalk.

(40) "Don't forget to come back and see our flying machine," Orville called after him.

(41) "Sure! You bet!" Lester said. (42) He was already halfway down the block.

(43) "He doesn't seem very interested," Wilbur said to his brother.

(44) "Well, no matter," Orville said with a smile. (45) "We'll always be remembered as the best bike mechanics in Dayton."

Name: _____   Date: _____

Two Bike Mechanics *(cont.)*

1   The meaning of sentence 3 is unclear. Which of the following would be the **BEST** replacement for sentence 3?

   A   Today was the day he'd been waiting for!

   B   Today was the day all of his hard work would pay off!

   C   Today was the day he'd hoped for!

   D   Today was the day finally!

---

2   Madison would like to change the word **busy** in sentence 4 to something that describes the situation more clearly. Which of the following would be the **BEST** replacement for the word *busy*?

   F   active

   G   occupied

   H   bustling

   J   speedy

---

3   What change needs to be made to sentence 10?

   A   Change *enter* to **entered**

   B   Change *pushed* to **push**

   C   Change *pushed* to **pushes**

   D   Change *open* to **opened**

Two Bike Mechanics *(cont.)*

4   What change, if any, should be made to sentence 12?

    F   Change *inches* to **inchs**

    G   Change *feet* to **foots**

    H   Change *skinny* to **skiny**

    J   No change is needed.

---

5   Which is the **BEST** verb to replace *looked* in sentence 14?

    A   smiled

    B   glanced

    C   frowned

    D   stared

---

6   What change, if any, should be made to sentence 25?

    F   Change *slightly* to **slightely**

    G   Change *totaly* to **totally**

    H   Change *taller* to **tallest**

    J   Make no change

The Best Yard Sale Ever

Directions: Read the selection and respond to the questions on pages 71–72.

Selma's teacher asked her class to write stories about dreams coming true. Selma wrote this story, but she wants it to be as good as possible before her teacher reads it. Read Selma's story and look for any errors. When you are finished reading, answer the questions that follow.

(1) "Whose going to want to buy this old junk?" Jessie Waldrip sneered.

(2) Karen gritted her teeth. (3) "We've sold plenty already," she replied.

(4) "That's right," Bonnie chimed in.

(5) It wasn't true, though. (6) They had made exactly $11.37. (7) They needed to raise more than $100 to buy tickets to see the hottest pop singer around, Tiffany Miller. (8) This yard sale was their only chance to raise the money.

(9) "Well," Jessie said, tossing her hair to one side, "I've got to go shopping now. (10) I need something to wear when I go see Tiffany in concert. (11) Bye-bye!"

(12) "I've got to go shopping now," Karen said, mimicking Jessie. (13) "Her parents buy her whatever she wants. (14) She doesn't know what it's like to work hard and earn your own money."

(15) "Who does she think she is?" Bonnie asked as she rearranged some old books on the card table.

GO ON

The Best Yard Sale Ever *(cont.)*

(16) "How much is this shirt? (17) Both girls looked up, startled. (18) They hadn't noticed a young woman who was looking through a rack of their old clothes. (19) She wore a large, floppy hat shoved down over her long, brown hair. (20) Her face was almost covered by a huge pair of sunglasses. (21) She held up one of Karen's old school T-shirts.

(22) "That's two dollars," Karen said.

(23) The young woman came over to the table, holding the shirt. (24) She stuck a hand in the pocket of her jeans. (25) "This is embarrassing," she said. (26) "I don't have any money. (27) Could I come back tomorrow?"

(28) "Sorry," Bonnie said. (29) "We need the money today. (30) We have to buy tickets to see Tiffany."

(31) "Tiffany Miller?" the young woman asked.

(32) "Yeah," Karen replied. (33) "We're her biggest fans."

(34) "Well, then," the young woman said with a smile. (35) "Would you trade the shirt for these?" (36) Out of her pocket she took two tickets and placed them on the table. (37) Then she took off her sunglasses. (38) Bonnie and Karen both gasped.

(39) "Ti. . Ti . . Tiffany!" they both screamed. (40) It really was their idol, Tiffany Miller.

(41) "So is it a trade?" Tiffany asked them.

(42) "You bet!" Karen shrieked. (43) She scooped up the tickets.

(44) "Good," Tiffany said. (45) "I'll see you at the concert. (46) You'll be able to recognize me there. (47) I'll be wearing your shirt."

The Best Yard Sale Ever *(cont.)*

1 What change should be made in sentence 1?

A Change *Whose* to **Who's**

B Change *to* to **too**

C Change *this* to **these**

D No change is needed.

---

2 Selma forgot to include an important detail in paragraph 4 (sentences 5–8).

> *The concert was that night, only a few hours away.*

Reread the paragraph carefully. Where is the **BEST** place to insert this sentence?

F After sentence 8

G After sentence 6

H Before sentence 7

J After sentence 5

---

3 What change, if any, should be made in sentence 8?

A Change *their* to **our**

B Change *This* to **That**

C Change *to* to **for**

D Make no change

GO ON

The Best Yard Sale Ever *(cont.)*

4 Which of these sentences can **BEST** follow and support sentence 15?

    F "I think all she cares about is clothes."

    G "I wonder what her outfit will look like."

    H "She thinks she's so much better than everyone else, but she never works for anything."

    J "I would never be friends with someone like that."

---

5 What change should be made in sentence 16?

    A Remove the quotation marks at the beginning

    B Replace the question mark with an exclamation point

    C Add a period at the end

    D Add quotation marks at the end

---

6 What change needs to be made in sentence 41?

    F Add a comma after *a*

    G Add a comma after *So*

    H Add a comma after the question mark

    J No change is needed in sentence 41.

Name: _____ Date: _____

Jabuti's Shell

Directions: Read the selection and respond to the questions on pages 75–76.

This Brazilian fable is about Jabuti, a clever turtle. Read Daniel's retelling of the fable, and see if you can find any errors Daniel made. When you finish reading, answer the questions that follow.

(1) Jabuti the turtle was the smartest of all the animals. (2) Everyone knew this. (3) He played a song on his flute that was as lovely as the wind. (4) The birds loved his music. (5) They all sang when he played. (6) Only the vulture didn't sing because he couldn't.

(7) Jabuti was very beautiful. (8) His shell was smooth and shiny. (9) The vulture's feathers were dark and dull. (10) His head was naked and pink. (11) The vulture was very jealous of Jabuti. (12) He tried to think of a way to take away Jabuti's song and his beauty. (13) Then, one day he saw his chance.

(14) The King of the Sky called all the birds together to sing. (15) The vulture heard that Jabuti wanted to go, too, but had no way to get up into the sky. (16) The vulture went to him. (17) "I may not be able to make music like you," the vulture said, "but I can spread my wings and soar. (18) Climb on my back, little friend."

Jabuti's Shell (cont.)

(19) They flew high above the treetops. (20) Suddenly, the vulture swooped and turned upside down. (21) The vulture did this on purpose. (22) Jabuti went tumbling down from the sky. (23) Crack! (24) He landed on a rock. (25) His smooth, shiny shell broke into pieces.

(26) The King of the Sky saw the vulture join the other birds. (27) "Where is Jabuti?" asked the King. (28) The vulture shrugged.

(29) The King of the Sky asked the birds to look for Jabuti. (30) They found him lying in the forest. (31) His beautiful shell was broken. (32) The King of the Sky told the birds to gather up the pieces. (33) Then he showed them how to patch Jabuti's shell back together. (34) As the birds touched the pieces of shell, they each became that color. (35) Each piece of Jabuti's shell was a different color. (36) Soon, Jabuti was in one piece again.

(37) The vulture flew down and saw what had happened. (38) "What about me?" he cried. (39) "Where is my beautiful color?"

(40) "You shouldn't have dropped Jabuti," the King of the Sky said. (41) So all the other birds got colors, but the vulture stayed as he was. (42) And he still can't sing.

(43) Moral: Beauty comes from the inside.

Jabuti's Shell *(cont.)*

1 What would be the **BEST** word to add before *music* in sentence 4?

    A loud

    B annoying

    C acceptable

    D wonderful

---

2 Daniel would like to rewrite sentence 7 to introduce the ideas in the second paragraph (sentences 7–13). Which of the following would be the **BEST** way to rewrite sentence 7?

    F Jabuti and his music were both beautiful.

    G The beauty of Jabuti's music matched the beauty of his shell.

    H Jabuti's music was beautiful and he was beautiful, too.

    J Jabuti was quite beautiful.

---

3 What would be the **BEST** word to replace *went* in sentence 16?

    A ran

    B flew

    C rushed

    D headed

Jabuti's Shell *(cont.)*

4   What is the most effective way for Daniel to combine sentences 20 and 21?

    F On purpose suddenly the vulture swooped and turned upside down.

    G Purposely and suddenly the vulture swooped and turned upside down.

    H He did this on purpose when suddenly the vulture swooped and turned upside down.

    J Suddenly—and on purpose—the vulture swooped and turned upside down.

---

5   What word should be added before *patch* in sentence 33?

    A gently

    B basically

    C actually

    D quickly

---

6   What word should be added before *flew* in sentence 37?

    F gently

    G directly

    H eventually

    J Make no change

STOP

Name: _____ Date: _____

The Scene from the Summit

Directions: Read the selection and respond to the questions on pages 79–80.

Christopher's teacher asked him to write an essay about a challenge he faced. Christopher needs you to read his paper and look for any corrections he needs to make. When you finish reading, answer the questions that follow.

(1) It seemed like a good idea at the time. (2) An afternoon hike would be fun, and at the top, we'd get a great view. (3) Two hours later, scrambling over slipery rocks in a light rain, I wasn't so sure.

(4) We were climbing Mount Saint Regis in Adirondack Park, near Saranac Lake, New York. (5) Workers at the visitor's center said the trail wasn't too hard. (6) Oh, yeah, they also said there'd be a great view from the top.

(7) At first, the trail was easy, just some gentle hills. (8) Then, after an hour, it started to climb pretty steeply. (9) Then we hit a stretch that seemed to go straight up. (10) Then it started to rain. (11) Soon my legs began to ache.

The Scene from the Summit (cont.)

(12) "The summit can't be too far," I said to myself. (13) About a half hour later, when we stopped to rest, I said it again. (14) I said it again fifteen minutes after that.

(15) "That view had better be worth it," I muttered. (16) Did I mention that we were promised a great view from the top?

(17) Then the trail leveled off. (18) It broke out of the trees. (19) We were walking over bare rock. (20) We were at the top. (21) On cue, the rain stopped and the sun came out.

(22) There it was, "The View." (23) We sat on the rocks and watched, not saying anything except, "Wow!" (24) It was, well, maybe you have to see it to understand. (25) Luckily, you can. (26) Take a look at the photo. (27) Was it worth the three-hour clime? (28) You tell me.

GO ON

The Scene from the Summit *(cont.)*

1 Which sentence is the **BEST** choice to insert before sentence 1?

  A Going for a hike is a fun experience.

  B I guess I was wrong.

  C Seeing a challenge through to the end can be a really rewarding experience.

  D Sometimes you don't know if an idea is any good until you try it.

---

2 What change needs to be made in sentence 3?

  F Change *light* to **lite**

  G Change *slipery* to **slippery**

  H Change *Two* to **Too**

  J No change is needed.

---

3 What word should replace *Then* in sentence 9?

  A Finally

  B After

  C Next

  D Now

The Scene from the Summit *(cont.)*

4   What change, if any, should be made in sentence 12?

    F   Change *myself* to **me**

    G   Change *to* to **at**

    H   Change *myself* to **oneself**

    J   No change should be made.

---

5   What is the **BEST** way to combine sentences 17 and 18?

    A   Then the trail leveled off, and it broke out of the trees.

    B   Then the trail leveled off and broke out of the trees.

    C   Then the trail leveled off, and it was breaking out of the trees.

    D   Then the trail leveled off, it broke out of the trees.

---

6   What change should be made in sentence 27?

    F   Change *hour* to **our**

    G   Change *hour* to **hours**

    H   Change *clime* to **climb**

    J   No change is needed in sentence 27.

Name: _____ Date: _____

Before He Changed the World

Directions: Read the selection and respond to the questions on pages 83–84.

Emma wrote this essay about Martin Luther King Jr. to describe what the great leader was like when he was a kid. Before she turns it in to her teacher, Emma would like you to read it to see if you can find any mistakes. After you are finished reading, answer the questions that follow.

(1) You know Martin Luther King Jr. as the legendary leader of the civil rights movement in the United States. (2) You may have heard at least part of his famous "I have a dream" speech. (3) But before Martin Luther King Jr. was a great leader, he was a little boy. (4) He went to school, played games, and played jokes on people.

(5) This description of King's childhood is in a book written by his big sister, Christine King Farris. (6) The book, called *my Brother Martin*, shows that Martin Luther King Jr. was in many ways a typical kid.

(7) Christine, Martin, and their little brother, Alfred, grew up in Atlanta, Georgia. (8) Their father, Martin Luther King Sr., was a minister. (9) Their mother, Alberta, was a musician. (10) To play board games and checkers is what the kids liked. (11) To play pranks they also liked. (12) For example, once they fooled their neighbors into thinking their grandmother's fur piece was a wild animal.

Before He Changed the World *(cont.)*

(13) There was lots of love in the King home. (14) But the world outside was often cruel. (15) Their parents tried to shield the children from the unfair laws that kept black and white people apart. (16) The Kings hardly ever took the kids to the movies because African Americans had to use a separate entrance to the theater and sit in the balcony.

(17) When they were young, the white children in the neighborhood played with the King children. (18) Then one day, when Martin was 7, the white kids said they could no longer play together. (19) Martin told his mother, "One day I'm going to turn this world upside down!"

(20) Martin, who was very smart, skipped grades 3 and 12. (21) He went to college when he was just 15. (22) By the time he was 25, he was a pastor of a church in Montgomery, Alabama. (23) He was only 26 when he became a leader of the Montgomery bus boycott in 1955. (24) African Americans in Montgomery refused to ride the buses as long as they had to sit in the back. (25) It was the first of many protests Martin would help lead.

GO ON

Before He Changed the World *(cont.)*

1   What change should be made in sentence 2?

   A   Capitalize *have*

   B   Capitalize *dream*

   C   Capitalize both *have* and *dream*

   D   No change needs to be made.

---

2   What change needs to be made in sentence 6?

   F   Change *book* to **Book**

   G   Change *my* to **My**

   H   Change *Brother* to **brother**

   J   No change is needed.

---

3   What is the correct way to write sentences 10 and 11?

   A   To play board games and checkers is what the kids liked. They also liked to play pranks.

   B   The kids liked to play board games and checkers. They also liked to play pranks.

   C   The kids liked to play board games and checkers. To play pranks they also liked.

   D   The kids liked board games and checkers to play. They also liked pranks to play.

Before He Changed the World *(cont.)*

4   Emma forgot to include an important detail in the fourth paragraph (sentences 13–16).

> *Some of the terrible laws of this time stated that black people could not eat in the same café as a white person, sit in the same taxi, or use the same drinking fountain.*

Reread the paragraph carefully. Where is the **BEST** place to insert this sentence?

F   After sentence 15

G   Before sentence 13

H   After sentence 16

J   After sentence 13

---

5   What change, if any, should be made in sentence 14?

A   Change *But* to **Then**

B   Change *often* to **never**

C   Change *But* to **And**

D   Make no change

---

6   Which sentence should Emma add to the end of her paper to bring it to a better close?

F   One of the other protests was the march on Washington.

G   The bus boycott was one of the civil rights movement's first victories.

H   Before he was done, he really did turn the world upside down.

J   He made great changes to our world.

Name: _____ Date: _____

Famous Hispanics

Directions: Read the selection and respond to the questions on pages 87–88.

Kwan wrote this paper about famous Hispanic Americans for his history class. He'd like you to read it and see if you can find any errors. When you finish reading Kwan's paper, answer the questions that follow.

David Farragut

(1) More than 30 million people living in the United States can trace their roots to Spain. (2) They are an important part of America's culture and history. (3) Here are just a handful of the Hispanic Americans who have made giant contributions to our country.

(4) **David Farragut**, naval hero, 1801–1870. (5) Farragut was the U.S. Navy's first four-star admiral. (6) In 1862, he was in charge of the Union fleet for the battle of New Orleans during the civil war. (7) It was Farragut who made the still famous remark, Damn the torpedoes, full speed ahead!

Famous Hispanics *(cont.)*

(8) **Ellen Ochoa**, astronaut, born 1958. (9) Ochoa has flown on four NASA space flights, and in space has spent 978 hours. (10) During one of her two visits to the International Space Station, she used the station's robotic arm to move goods from the space shuttle to the station.

(11) **César Chávez**, labor leader, 1927–1993. (12) Chávez was a migrant farmworker who started the United Farm Workers union in the 1960s. (13) The UFW fought for better pay and working conditions for thousands of farmworkers in the U.S.

(14) **Luis Alvarez**, physicist, 1911–1988. (15) Alvarez was part of the team of scientists who built the first atomic bomb during World War II. (16) In 1968, he won the Nobel Prize in Physics for his scientific work.

(17) **Isabel Allende**, writer, born 1942. (18) Allende is the author of several books, as well as plays and stories for children. (19) Her novel *The House of Spirits* was made into a movie in 1994.

(20) **Alex Rodriguez**, baseball player, born 1975. (21) Rodriguez, also known as A-Rod, is one of the best all-around players in baseball. (22) In 1998, he became the third player ever to hit 40 home runs and steal 40 bases in the same season.

Famous Hispanics *(cont.)*

1 David forgot to include an important detail in the first paragraph (sentences 1–3).

> *In many parts of the United States, Hispanics make up a large part of the*
> *population.*

Reread the paragraph carefully. Where is the **BEST** place to insert this sentence?

A After sentence 1

B Before sentence 1

C After sentence 2

D After sentence 3

2 Which changes should be made in sentence 6?

F Capitalize *civil*

G Capitalize *battle*

H Capitalize *war*

J Capitalize *civil*, *battle*, and *war*

3 What change needs to be made to sentence 7?

A Remove the comma after *remark*

B Add quotation marks before *Damn* and after the exclamation point

C Change the exclamation point to a question mark

D No change needs to be made.

GO ON

Famous Hispanics (cont.)

4 What change needs to be made to sentence 9?

   F On four NASA space flights Ochoa has flown, and has spent 978 hours in space.

   G Ochoa has flown on four NASA space flights and has spent 978 hours in space.

   H On four NASA space flights Ochoa has flown, and in space has spent 978 hours.

   J No change needs to be made.

---

5 Which is the **BEST** way to start sentence 16?

   A Next, in 1968

   B Finally, in 1968

   C Meanwhile, in 1968

   D No change should be made.

---

6 Kwan's paper ends abruptly. Which sentence should Kwan add to the end of his paper to bring it to a better close?

   F A-Rod played 22 seasons in Major League Baseball for the Seattle Mariners, Texas Rangers, and New York Yankees.

   G These are some important Hispanic Americans.

   H These amazing people are just a few of the Hispanics who have made great contributions in many fields throughout history.

   J In many parts of the United States, Hispanics make up a large part of the population.

Name: _____ Date: _____

My Friend, the Genius

Directions: Read the selection and respond to the questions on pages 91–92.

Abigail's teacher told the class they had to write a paper describing a friend. Abigail wrote this paper about her friend Matt, who is an amazing jazz musician even though he is only 11. Abigail would like you to read her paper to see if you can find any errors. When you are finished reading, answer the questions that follow.

(1) Okay, I have to admit it. (2) My best friend Matt is a genius. (3) What else can you say about an 11-year-old kid who has his own jazz band?

(4) It all started when Matt Savage was just 6. (5) He couldn't play with toys like other kids his age. (6) No, Matt went and taught himself to read music! (7) It seemed as if he just knew how to play the piano without being taught. (8) He did spend a lot of time practicing, though.

(9) It wasn't long before he was writing his own songs. (10) Jazz is not really my favorite kind of music, and you can tell that Matt's songs are good. (11) The one I like the most is called "Shuffling the Cards."

My Friend, the Genius *(cont.)*

(12) That jazz band I mentioned isn't made up of a bunch of kids playing in a garage. (13) Matt plays with two adult musicians. (14) They play in real jazz clubs, and people pay to see them. (15) They've even recorded a couple of albums. (16) The bass player is named John, and he's 36. (17) I asked him what it's like to have an 11-year-old for a boss. (18) "It's weird," John told me, "but it's fun playing with a kid who's really good."

(19) Matt seems to hear music differently than most people. (20) Most of us hear the whole band at once. (21) But he seems to be able to hear both every instrument and every note. (22) "A piano is like 88 instruments combined in one," he says. (23) "Each key has its own sound."

(24) Matt is kind of a local celebrity. (25) It seems that everyone in our town of Manchester, New Hampshire, knows Matt or has heard of him. (26) And most everyone is proud of his musical ability and celebrity status.

(27) Still, with all that attention he's not at all stuck up. (28) Aside from the genius music skills, he's just a kid, like me. (29) Yeah, I have to admit it, he may be a genius, but he's also really cool.

My Friend, the Genius *(cont.)*

1 What word should be added before *play with toys* in sentence 5?

    A occasionally

    B just

    C carefully

    D rarely

---

2 What change, if any, needs to be made in sentence 10?

    F Change *music* to **Music**

    G Change *and* to **but**

    H Change *kind* to **kinds**

    J No change is needed.

---

3 What is the most effective way to combine sentences 14 and 15?

    A They play in real jazz clubs where people pay to see them, and they've even recorded a couple of albums.

    B People pay to see them play in real jazz clubs, so they've even recorded a couple of albums.

    C People pay to see them play in real jazz clubs, and they've even recorded a couple of albums.

    D They play in real jazz clubs, people pay to see them, and they've even recorded a couple of albums.

My Friend, the Genius *(cont.)*

4   What change, if any, needs to be made to sentence 21?

    F Change *both* to **neither**

    G Change *But* to **So**

    H Change *note* to **notes**

    J No change needs to be made.

---

5   Abigail forgot to include an important detail in paragraph 6 (sentences 24–26).

> It is obvious that I am one of those proud people. Otherwise, I wouldn't be writing about him.

Reread the paragraph carefully. Where is the **BEST** place to insert these sentences?

    A Before sentence 24

    B Before sentence 25

    C After sentence 25

    D After sentence 26

---

6   What change should be made in sentence 27?

    F Add a comma after *he's*

    G Remove the comma after *Still*

    H Add a comma after *attention*

    J Make no change

Name: _____   Date: _____

Free All the Orcas

Directions: Read the selection and respond to the questions on pages 95–96.

Angel wrote this letter in order to persuade others not to keep orcas locked up in captivity. His teacher said she would send it to the big aquariums if the letter was well written. Angel needs you to read his letter and help him fix any mistakes. After you finish reading, answer the questions that follow.

(1) Dear Sir or Madam,

(2) I am writing to object to orcas living in theme parks or aquariums. (3) Keeping orcas in captivity is cruel and should not be allowed.

(4) I understand that people enjoy seeing orcas do tricks at theme parks. (5) Orcas in aquariums can help people learn more about these wonderful animals. (6) However, even in the best condishins, being kept in a pen is bad for the orcas. (7) No amount of enjoyment or education is worth the suffering it causes them.

(8) An adult killer whale, or orca, might be 25 feet long and weigh about 12,000 pounds. (9) In the wild, they travel thousands of miles in the ocean. (10) They live in large groups called pods, which might contain as many as 20 other orcas. (11) They hunt seals, fish, and dolphins.

(12) Compare that to life for orcas in a theme park. (13) They often live alone, without the company of other orcas. (14) The pools they are kept in are often very small. (15) They may not receive proper medical care.

Free All the Orcas *(cont.)*

(16) The most famous example of a captive orca is Keiko. (17) Keiko was the orca who starred in the movie *Free willy*. (18) Keiko had been captured in the waters near Iceland when he was two. (19) At the time of the movie, Keiko was living in an aquarium in Mexico. (20) His skin was covered in sores. (21) The fin on his back, called the dorsal fin, flopped over. (22) Keiko was sick.

(23) After the movie came out and people found out about Keiko, they came to his rescue. (24) A group called the Free Willy Keiko Foundation moved Keiko to a seawater pool in Oregon. (25) During the next year, Keiko grew healthy. (26) In 2002, he was released in the waters off of Iceland. (27) He joined a wild pod and swam more than 1,000 miles to Norway. (28) Keiko died in 2003, but he had spent his last year as a healthy free orca.

(29) Orcas are graceful, smart animals. (30) The next time you see one in a pool at a theme park, ask ourselves, "Is it okay to pen up an intelligent animal just so people can have fun watching it?"

(31) I think you will agree that the answer is "no."

(32) Sincerely,

(33) Angel Edmunds

Free All the Orcas *(cont.)*

1 What change needs to be made in sentence 6?

  A Change *kept* to **keeped**

  B Change *pen* to **penn**

  C Change *condishins* to **conditions**

  D No change is needed in sentence 6.

---

2 Angel would like to add a sentence to the sixth paragraph (sentences 16–22) to better explain the ideas in this paragraph. Which of the following would be the **BEST** sentence to add just before sentence 20?

  F Just behind the dorsal fin is a patch of gray called a saddle because it looks like a riding saddle.

  G His pool was too small and too warm.

  H The movie is set in the Pacific Northwest.

  J His pool wasn't good.

---

3 What change, if any, needs to be made in sentence 17?

  A Change *willy* to **Willy**

  B Change *Free* to **free**

  C Change *orca* to **Orca**

  D No change is needed in this sentence.

Free All the Orcas *(cont.)*

4   What is the most effective way for Angel to combine sentences 25 and 26?

    F During the next year, Keiko grew healthy, and in 2002 he was released in the waters off of Iceland.

    G During the next year, Keiko grew healthy, but in 2002 he was released in the waters off of Iceland.

    H In 2002, he was released in the waters off of Iceland because during the next year, Keiko grew healthy.

    J In 2002, he was released in the waters off of Iceland, however during the next year Keiko grew healthy.

---

5   What change should be made in sentence 28?

    A Add a comma after *healthy*

    B Change the period to an exclamation point

    C Remove the comma after *2003*

    D No change is needed in sentence 28.

---

6   How should sentence 30 be changed?

    F Change *park* to **parks**

    G Change *ourselves* to **yourself**

    H Change *in* to **on**

    J Change *at* to **on**

Name: _____ Date: _____

Money Isn't Everything... or Is It?

Directions: Read the selection and respond to the questions on pages 99–100.

Samantha was excited to write this paper for her math class. Her paper describes one baseball team's approach to hiring players. The team uses math instead of spending the most money. Samantha would like you to read it and see if you can find any mistakes before she turns it in. When you are finished reading, answer the questions that follow.

(1) Can you buy a championship with money? (2) Most baseball fans would say "yes. (3) All you have to do is look at the New York Yankees. (4) The Yankees' former owner, George Steinbrenner, spent millions to hire the best players in baseball. (5) The Yankees have the largest payroll in baseball. (6) In 2003, it was about $158 million. (7) Can money buy success? (8) Well, the Yankees have been in the playoffs an amazing 19 out of the last 23 years.

(9) But recently, some person in baseball have been saying that money isn't everything. (10) They insist that you can win in baseball without spending out-of-this-world sums. (11) Billy Beane, the executive vice president of the Oakland Athletics (the A's), has been the leader in this new approach to winning. (12) Beane says a different approach helps him make decisions. (13) Guess what? (14) The best player isn't always the most expensive.

Money Isn't Everything… or Is It? *(cont.)*

(15) Beane's math rates a player who gets on bass much higher than one who hits a lot of homers. (16) That's why the A's don't have a home-run king like Barry Bonds. (17) It's also why first baseman Scott Hatteberg fits right in. (18) Hatteberg is not a power hitter, but he has a high on-base percentage.

(19) The A's have become one of the best teams in the American League. (20) At the same time, the A's spend far less on players' salaries than many other teams do. (21) Now other teams, including the Boston Red Sox and the Toronto Blue Jays are borrowing Beane's math.

(22) There's only one problem. (23) In 2004, the A's, the Red Sox, and the Blue Jays all failed to win a pennant. (24) The A's came close, just one game behind Anaheim. (25) The Blue Jays finished last in their division. (26) The Red Sox managed to get the wild card after losing their division to guess who? (27) That's right, the Yankees.

(28) No one is saying Beane's ideas are all wrong. (29) It's clear they have helped the A's. (30) Maybe one day his team will even win the World Series. (31) But, like it or not, money still counts in the major leagues. (32) Which is good news—if you're a Yankees fan.

Money Isn't Everything... or Is It? *(cont.)*

1 What change needs to be made in sentence 2?

A Add quotation marks at the end of the sentence

B Remove the quotation marks before *yes*

C Add a comma after *fans*

D No change is needed in sentence 2.

---

2 How does sentence 9 need to be changed?

F Change *person* to **persons**

G Change *person* to **people**

H Change *recently* to **recentliy**

J No change should be made.

---

3 Samantha wants to strengthen the focus of her story. Which of the following is the **BEST** replacement for sentence 12?

A Beane says a different approach helps him decide which players to hire.

B Beane says a scientific approach using math helps him make decisions.

C Beane says a scientific approach using math helps him decide which players to hire.

D Beane says a better approach helps him make important decisions.

Money Isn't Everything... or Is It? *(cont.)*

4   What change, if any, needs to be made in sentence 15?

    F   Change *bass* to **base**

    G   Change *homers* to **hommers**

    H   Change *one* to **won**

    J   Make no change

---

5   The meaning of sentence 18 is unclear. Which sentence can Samantha use to replace sentence 18?

    A   Hatteberg scores often.

    B   Hatteberg is not a power hitter, but his teammates hit well.

    C   Even though Hatteberg doesn't score many home runs, he gets on base often.

    D   Hatteberg does not have a higher than average ability in terms of his batting, but he has a high on-base percentage.

---

6   What change needs to be made in sentence 21?

    F   Remove the comma after *teams*

    G   Change *teams* to **team's**

    H   Add a comma after *Jays*

    J   Change *Beane's* to **Beanes'**

Name: _____ Date: _____

A New Game

Directions: Read the selection and respond to the questions on pages 103–104.

Juan wrote this review of the game Bop It Extreme 2 for the school newspaper. Juan would like you to read it and find any mistakes before he gives it to his editor. When you finish reading, answer the questions that follow.

Bop It Extreme 2 by Hasbro, about $25

(1) Confeshion: This review almost didn't get written. (2) We were having so much fun playing Bop It Extreme 2 that I didn't want to put the game down to write. (3) Finally, someone grabbed it out of my hands. (4) So while I'm waiting for my turn again, I'll try to write something—quick!

(5) I'll start by trying to describe what it looks like. (6) Bop It is a uniquely strange-looking gadget. (7) The game is a plastic, one-piece, electronic, toy shaped sort of like the letter *S*. (8) At the ends and on the curves there are four different movable gizmos. (9) In the center is a large round button.

(10) Once you start playing, an annoying man's voice starts quickly calling out commands. (11) "Flick it!" (12) "Twist it!" (13) "Spin it!" (14) "Pull it!" (15) Each command is matched to one of the four gizmos. (16) For example, if the voice says, "Twist it!" you're supposed to twist a yellow knob at one of the corners of the game. (17) If the voice yells, "Bop it!" you hit the round button in the center. (18) The commands come in random order, so you don't know what you have to do next.

A New Game *(cont.)*

(19) When the voice calls out commands, you have to act in a split second. (20) For some reason, the first 20 times it said, "Spin it!" I hit the twist knob instead. (21) I did get the hang of it finally. (22) You have to really pay attention, though. (23) I know that it's just a computer chip, but it seemed to me that little voice was really out to trick me.

(24) There are three different ways to play. (25) You can play solo, take turns, or play in teams of two. (26) Either you love playing in teams or you hate it, you will have a fun challenge with four people all trying to hang on to the game at the same time.

(27) As you can tell, I really enjoyed the game. (28) I do have a warning, though: It seems like the kind of game you might play for a couple of days straight and then never touch again. (29) I promise to write an update if that happens. (30) If you don't hear from me again, it means I'm too busy trying to "Twist it!", "Spin It!", "Pull it!", or "Flick it!"

GO ON

A New Game *(cont.)*

1   What change should be made to sentence 1?

   A   Change *written* to **writen**

   B   Change *get* to **got**

   C   Change *Confeshion* to **Confession**

   D   Remove the apostrophe from **didn't**

---

2   What change, if any, should be made in sentence 7?

   F   Change *game* to **Game**

   G   Add a comma after **a**

   H   Remove the comma after *electronic*

   J   Change *plastic* to **plastick**

---

3   What change, if any, needs to be made in sentence 18?

   A   Change *commands* to **comands**

   B   Change *random* to **randdom**

   C   Change *know* to **now**

   D   Make no change

A New Game (cont.)

4 Juan forgot to include an important detail in the fourth paragraph (sentences 19–23).

> *I'm not sure why, but messing up that many times in a row really made me determined to keep playing until I won.*

Reread the paragraph carefully. Where is the **BEST** place to insert this sentence?

  F After sentence 21

  G After sentence 20

  H After sentence 19

  J After sentence 23

---

5 How does sentence 26 need to be changed?

  A Change *will have* to **have had**

  B Change *Either* to **Whether**

  C Change *hate* to **hated**

  D No change needs to be made.

---

6 Which sentence should Juan add to the end of his review to bring it to a better close?

  F This review recommends Bop It Extreme 2 as a fun game.

  G You can find information online that can help you change the speed of Bop It Extreme 2.

  H In the meantime, why don't you take my recommendation and give Bop It Extreme 2 a try?

  J The high score of Bop It Extreme 2 is 250.

Otters: River or Sea?

A Compare and Contrast Book
by Cathleen McConnell

Otters are mustelids. Mustelids have long bodies, short legs, round ears, and thick fur. Other members of the mustelid family include skunks, badgers, ferrets, fishers, and wolverines.

skunk

badgers

ferret

fisher

wolverine

There are 13 species of otters. Most are river otters that live near water but spend much of their time on land.

One type of river otter, the marine otter, is found along the Pacific coast of South America. These otters may swim in the ocean briefly to hunt.

African Clawless Otter
Aonyx capensis

Asian Small-Clawed Otter
Aonyx cinereus

Congo Clawless Otter
Aonyx congicus

Eurasian Otter
Lutra lutra

Giant Otter
Pteronura brasiliensis

Hairy Nosed Otter
Lutra sumatrana

Neotropical Otter
Lontra longicaudis

North American River Otter
Lontra canadensis

Smooth Coated Otter
Lutrogale perspicillata

Southern River Otter
Lontra provocax

Spotted-Necked Otter
Lutra maculicollis

Marine Otter
Lontra felina

Sea Otter
Enhydra lutris

Sea otters are the only otters that are truly adapted to the marine environment. They can sleep, eat, mate, and give birth, without ever coming to shore.

What can the name of some of the species tell you about that animal?

River otters live near a variety of aquatic habitats including rivers, ponds, lakes, and even the ocean.

They move well on land and in water. When a predator approaches on land, a river otter rushes to the water to escape.

Sea otters live in the Pacific Ocean. They are often seen floating on their backs, sometimes wrapped in kelp.

Sea otters completely depend on the sea for their survival.

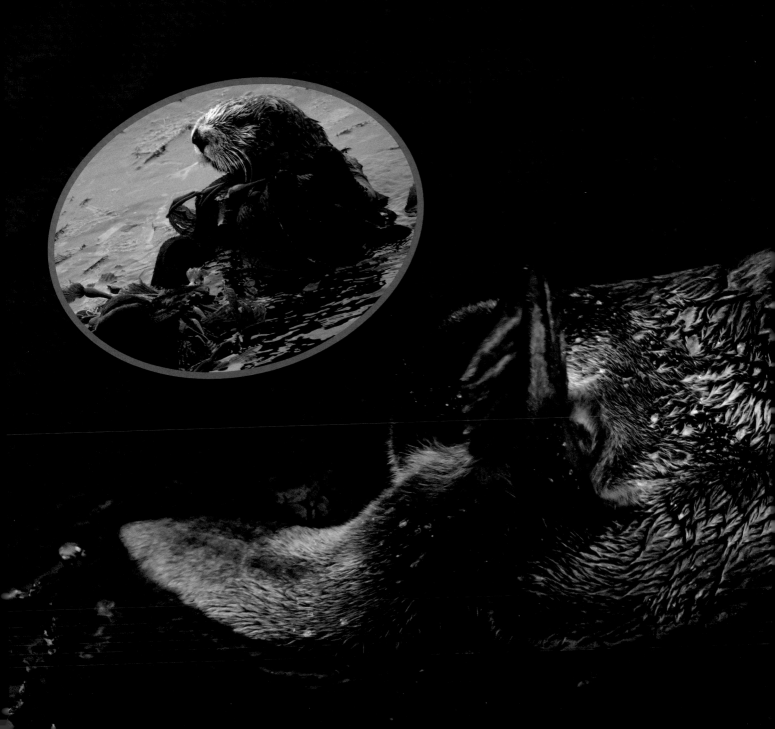

River otters use their strong tails and webbed feet to dive and to rocket themselves through the water.

They can hold their breath for up to two minutes as they chase their underwater prey.

Sea otters use their large tails and back flippers to dive, swim, and steer as they float on the surface.

They can hold their breath for up to five minutes and dive as deep as 250 feet (76 meters) to hunt for food.

River otters use their sensitive whiskers to find, chase, and catch fast-moving underwater prey.

Sea otters use their bristly mustaches to sense still or slow-moving prey hiding on rocks, kelp, or the seafloor.

River otters use their front feet to hold their food. They have sharp teeth to grab slippery prey.

Sea otters eat while floating on their backs, using their chest as a table. They use their flat molars to crush the hard shells of their prey. If a shell is very thick, they will use a rock or other hard tool to crack it open.

River otters eat fish, frogs, reptiles, small mammals, birds, eggs, and aquatic invertebrates like crayfish.

Most river otters have claws to grab prey and to help them move on land.

Sea otters eat crabs, sea urchins, snails, clams, abalone, and other invertebrates.

Sea otters have thick paw pads to hold pokey sea urchins or pinching crabs.

River otters' fur keeps them warm in and out of the water.

They can also stay warm and dry by curling up with each other in a den or other shelter on land.

Sea otters have the thickest fur of any animal. Unlike other marine mammals, they don't have a layer of blubber to keep them warm.

Just like you might wear a puffy coat outside when it's cold, they blow air into their fur for extra insulation.

River otters spend much of their day marking territory. They will scratch and rub their scent glands on rocks and trees.

Sea otters spend a large part of their day grooming their fur. If they don't keep their fur clean, they won't stay warm in their cold ocean habitat.

North American river otters tend to live alone or in pairs. They will often play with other otters they meet.

Some river otter species may live in large families of over ten individuals. One name for a group of river otters is a romp.

A group of sea otters is called a raft and can have up to 1,000 otters!

When watching a raft of sea otters, you may see some wrapped up in the kelp or holding paws to stay together.

Depending on the species, a river otter mom could have between one and six pups in a litter.

The pups will live with their mother and siblings until they are between a year and 18 months.

Sea otter moms usually have one pup at a time. Sea otter pups can't swim or dive when they are born. They can only float. A sea otter mom may wrap the pup in kelp to keep it safe when she hunts for food.

Sea otters have to learn a lot from their mothers and will stay with them for eight months or longer.

For Creative Minds

Otter Math

Common Name	size inches	size cm	weight US	weight metric
African Clawless Otter	42-63 in	115-160 cm	26-42 lb	12-19 kg
Asian Small-Clawed Otter	25-37 in	65-94 cm	4-11 lb	2-5 kg
Congo Clawless Otter	43-59 in	110-150 cm	26-37 lb	12-17 kg
Eurasian Otter	42-54 in	102-138 cm	9-24 lb	4-11 kg
Giant Otter	57-71 in	145-180 cm	53-84 lb	24-38 kg
Hairy Nosed Otter	41-44 in	105-113 cm	11-17 lb	5-8 kg
Neotropical Otter	35-53 in	90-136 cm	22-31 lb	10-14 kg
North American River Otter	39-60 in	100-153 cm	18-24 lb	8-11 kg
Smooth Coated Otter	42-51 in	106-130 cm	15-22 lb	7-10 kg
South American River Otter	39-46 in	100-116 cm	11-22 lb	5-10 kg
Spotted-Necked Otter	37-45 in	95-115 cm	9-15 lb	4-7 kg
Marine Otter	34-45 in	87-115 cm	7-13 lb	3-6 kg
Southern Sea Otter	48 in avg	114 cm avg	45-65 lb	20-29 kg
Northern Sea Otter	60 in avg	153 cm avg	50-100 lb	23-45 kg

In general, male otters are longer and heavier than female otters. Shown sizes and weight conversions are rounded. Body length includes tails.

Use the chart to answer the questions below:

- **Which otter species is about your size?**
- **Which otter species is about your weight?**
- **Which otter species is the largest? Smallest?**

The sizes are given in inches. Do you know how many inches are in a foot? Pick an otter and convert the inches to feet and inches.

Select an otter species and find items that weigh the same or similar amount. Use two columns to make a list of the comparisons you made.

How tall are the adults you know? If you don't know, you can ask one or look up the height of a famous adult. Are there any otter species longer than their height?

Adaptations

1: webbed front feet with claws

2: flat molars to break shells

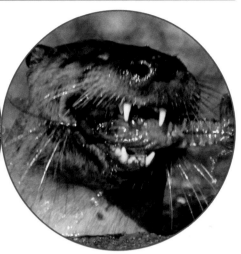

3: sharp teeth to hold prey

4: large, webbed back flippers

5: padded front paws to hold sharp prey

6: wrap themselves in kelp to stay in one place

Adaptations help animals survive in their habitats. *Which of these adaptations would you find on a river otter? Which belong to sea otters?*

Physical adaptations are body parts. Behavioral adaptations are things they do. *Can you identify which of these adaptations are behavioral?*

Answers:
River Otters: 1 Most, but not all, river otters have claws on their front feet. They all have some type of webbing between their toes. 3.
Sea Otters: 2. 4. 5. 6.
Behavioral: 6

Fun Facts

All 13 species of otters are on the IUCN Red List of Threatened Species. Like many animals, one of the leading threats to otter populations is a loss of habitat due to human development and other activities. Some species of otters are still hunted for their fur. Sea otter populations are vulnerable to oil spills from large ships and tankers that travel near their coastal habitats. Otter species are sensitive to many kinds of pollution in the water and on land.

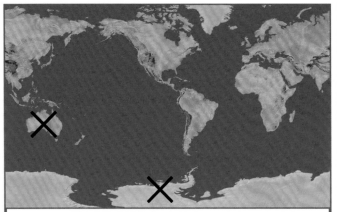

Otters are found on all continents except Australia and Antarctica.

All otters have some type of webbing on their feet. Webbed feet help animals move through the water.

Which of these girls do you think will move faster through the water? Why?

Sea otters have special "pockets" under their arms to hold food as they hunt for more. They may also carry around their favorite rock or other tool for smashing the shells of their prey.

What kind of tools do you use to prepare and eat your food?

When chasing prey, river otters can hold their breath underwater for up to 2 minutes. Sea otters can hold their breath for up to 5 minutes.

How long can you hold your breath?

Sea otters need to eat around 25% of their body weight each day. River otters need to eat about 15% of their body weight each day. *How much would you need to eat if you were a sea or river otter?*

Sea otters can have up to 1,000,000 hairs in one square inch on their body.

River otters can have up to 450,000 hairs per square inch.

Humans average 2,200 hairs per square inch on their head.

one square inch

Otter Enrichment at Zoos and Aquariums

Otters and other mustelids are known for being very clever. When they are under human care at a zoo or aquarium, their caretakers must be very creative to come up with items for them to interact with, and activities to keep their minds busy and encourage natural behaviors. This is called providing **enrichment**.

Enrichment can be something as simple as a toy or special treat. Learning something new or fun during a training session can also be a form of enrichment.

Training is a very important part of caring for animals. For example, an otter can learn to move onto a scale to be weighed. Losing or gaining weight can be a sign that something might be wrong. Having this information helps keepers make important health decisions.

Zookeepers do all kinds of things to keep the otters in their care happy and healthy. They might make an "ice treat" by freezing a Jell-O mold full of water and clams. Otters love to smash the ice to get to the food frozen inside.

What do you think a sea otter would do if you gave it some cloth strips from a car wash? Use it like kelp to wrap themselves in, of course!

Have you ever provided enrichment for your pet? If you give them toys and play with them, that is enrichment. Cats love playing in old boxes or chasing things as though they are hunting. Many dogs may be happy chasing a stick or an old ball.

Thanks to Christine Schmitz, Curator of Education at Utah's Hogle Zoo for giving me my first "real" job at an aquarium and to Everett Athorp who took me to see my first wild sea otters.—CM

Thanks to Lesley Wright of the International Union for Conservation of Nature (IUCN) Otter Specialists Group for verifying the accuracy of the information in this book.

With the exception of the specific photographs listed below, all photographs are licensed through Adobe Stock Photos or Shutterstock. Thanks to Ingrid Barrentine and Zach Hawn for the use of their sea otter enrichment photographs. And thanks to the following members of the International Union for Conservation of Nature (IUCN) Otter Specialists Group (www.otterspecialistgroup.org) and the International Otter Survival Fund (www.otter.org) for sharing their otter species images:

African Clawless	*Aonyx capensis*	Rowan Jordaan
Eurasian Otter	*Lutra lutra*	Henry Krüger
Neotropical Otter	*Lontra longicaudis*	Nicole Duplaix
Hairy-Nosed Otter	*Lutra sumatrana*	Nicole Duplaix
Southern River Otter	*Lontra provocax*	Jose Luis Bartheld
Spotted-Necked Otter	*Hydrictis maculicollis*	Jan Reed-Smith
Marine Otter	*Lontra felina Gonzalo*	Henry Krüger
Congo Clawless	*Aonyx congicus*	Rita and Glen Chapman

Library of Congress Cataloging-in-Publication Data

Names: McConnell, Cathleen, 1966- author.
Title: Otters : river or sea? : a compare and contrast book / by Cathleen
  McConnell.
Description: Mt. Pleasant : Arbordale Publishing, LLC, [2021] | Includes
  bibliographical references.
Identifiers: LCCN 2021013705 (print) | LCCN 2021013706 (ebook) | ISBN
  9781643519784 (paperback) | ISBN 9781638170167 (adobe pdf) | ISBN
  9781638170358 (epub) | ISBN 9781643519975 (Interactive, dual-language,
  read-aloud ebook)
Subjects: LCSH: Otters--Juvenile literature. | North American river
  otter--Juvenile literature. | Sea otter--Juvenile literature.
Classification: LCC QL737.C25 M35 2021 (print) | LCC QL737.C25 (ebook) |
  DDC 599.769--dc23
LC record available at https://lccn.loc.gov/2021013705
LC ebook record available at https://lccn.loc.gov/2021013706

Bibliography

Bibliography
"Enhydra lutis". Animal Diversity Web. University of Michigan Museum of Zoology. www.animaldiversity.org.
Love, John A. (1992). *Sea Otters*. Golden, Colorado: Fulcrum Publishing.
"How to Tell the Difference between Sea Otters and River Otters." Ocean Conservancy, 30 Jan. 2019, oceanconservancy.org.
"IOSF." www.otter.org/Public/.
"Marine Otter." Oceana, 2019, oceana.org/marine-life/marine-mammals/marine-otter.
"North American River Otter." National Wildlife Federation, 2019, www.nwf.org.
"North American River Otter." Smithsonian's National Zoo, 25 Apr. 2016, nationalzoo.si.edu.
"Northern Sea Otter Species Profile, River Otter Species Profile, Alaska Department of Fish and Game." www.adfg.alaska.gov.
"Otter Species." IUCN Otter Specialist Group, www.otterspecialistgroup.org.
Reed-Smith, Jan. Email Interview.
"Sea Otters | Seattle Aquarium." 20 Nov. 2012, www.seattleaquarium.org.
Species - Otter Facts and Information. www.otter-world.com.
"Southern Sea Otter." Georgia Aquarium, 2019, www.georgiaaquarium.org.

Lexile Level: 990L

Printed in the US
This product conforms to CPSIA 2008
First Printing

Arbordale Publishing, LLC
Mt. Pleasant, SC 29464
www.ArbordalePublishing.com